Write it in Arabic

A Workbook and Step-by-Step
Guide to Writing the Arabic Alphabet

Fun with Arabic

Library and Archives Canada Cataloguing in Publication

Ghali, Naglaa
        Write it in Arabic : a workbook and step-by-step guide to writing the Arabic alphabet / Naglaa Ghali.

Text in English and Arabic.
ISBN 0-9730512-1-3

        1. Arabic alphabet. 2. Arabic language—Writing. 3. Arabic language—Vocabulary. 4. Arabic language—Problems, exercises, etc. 5. Arabic language—Textbooks for second language learners—English speakers. I. Title.

PJ6123.G43 2004   492.781'3   C2004-903547-9

This book was printed in Canada.

    2 3 4 5   08 07 06 05

All inquiries should be addressed to
info@funwitharabic.com
http://www.funwitharabic.com

Contents

Preface

The Arabic Language

Before You Start

Part One

Letters and Numbers

alif	7
baa', taa', and thaa'	8
geem, Haa', and khaa'	10
Notes and Review: *First Set of Letters*	12
daal and dhaal	14
raa' and zaay	16
seen and sheen	18
Saad and Daad	20
Taa' and Zaa'	22
Notes and Review: *Second Set of Letters*	24
'ayn	26
ghayn	28
faa' and qaaf	30
kaaf	32
laam	34
Notes and Review: *The Prefix alef laam*	36
meem	38
noon	40
haa'	42
waaw	44
yaa'	46

hamza   48

taa' marbouta   50

Vowel Marks   52

Numbers   54

Handwriting   58
Notes on Handwriting   59

Part Two

Exercises   64

Answers   106

Afterword   108

Preface

Write it in Arabic is an alphabet guide and workbook that offers a hands-on approach to learning Arabic. Away from lengthy introductions and linguistic complications, this book will lead you directly into unravelling the mystery of the Arabic script and learning how to read and write it.

In this book, you will be introduced to the Arabic alphabet in sequence. You will practice writing the shape of each letter and you will learn how to join the letters to form words. This book will also guide you in the pronunciation of the different letters of the alphabet. You should become familiar with the shape and sound of each letter before moving on to the next one.

The words provided in the exercises have been carefully selected to help you practice the letters that you have already learned, while enriching your vocabulary. A set of easy-to-follow exercises is also included in Part Two. These exercises are designed to help you practice the Arabic style of writing and teach you new, frequently used, Arabic words.

By the end of the workbook, you should have a strong grasp of the Arabic alphabet and knowledge of its shape and sound. This will assist you greatly in further Arabic studies.

The Arabic Language

Arabic is spoken by more than 250 million people in over 22 countries. It is the official language of all Arab countries, hence forming a cultural bond among them. Arabic belongs to the Semitic group of languages which includes Hebrew, Aramaic, Ethiopic and others.

There are three basic forms of the language: classical, modern, and colloquial. The classical form is the language of old literary Arabic and the Arabic of the Qu'ran. The modern standard Arabic is the written and official language of the Arab world today. The colloquial form is the commonly spoken Arabic, which differs greatly from one country to another. Written Arabic, however, remains the same throughout the Arab world. The Arabic alphabet has also been adopted, with some modifications, by non-Semitic languages, including Persian, Urdu, Malay, and Pashto.

This workbook will introduce you to the modern standard Arabic, which is the written language of the Arab world today. Although this form is not the commonly spoken language, it is widely understood in all Arab countries, and shares several similarities with classical Arabic. You might sound out of place if you try to converse in modern standard Arabic, since the colloquial form is usually spoken. Nevertheless, this is the proper form of the language. The purpose of this book is to provide you with the basic skills for reading, writing, and understanding Arabic as it appears in newspapers, current literature, and educational materials.

Before You Start

The Arabic alphabet consists of 28 letters. The letters are written from right to left. To remain faithful to Arabic written work, this book opens like any book printed in Arabic. As well, you will write from right to left when completing the exercises.

When you write in Arabic, you join the letters together to form words. The shape of most letters changes according to their position in a word. There are, however, six letters that never change shape. In this book, we will refer to them as "disjoined letters." These letters do not join the letters following them and their shape does not change according to their position in a word. Joined letters, on the other hand, join the letters on their left and right. Most joined letters have more than one form. The short form of the letter is used at the beginning of a word or when it falls between two other joined letters. The long form is used when the letter falls at the end of a word or when it stands alone.

To complete the exercises in this workbook, start at the dot and follow the arrows. Try your best not to lift your pen when writing. Start with the basic shape of the letter, and then place any additional dots or strokes. Remember, any additional marks are placed from right to left. Pay attention to the writing line, and note which parts of the letter belong above or beneath the line. Do not confuse the name of the letter with its pronunciation. In Arabic, the name of the letter does not necessarily correspond to the sound it produces.

3

Part One

Letters and Numbers

alif

alif

The *alif* is the first letter of the Arabic alphabet. It is a disjoined letter. This means that it does not join the letter following it. It does, however, join the letter preceding it, that is, the letter to its right. The *alif* is written as a vertical stroke from top to bottom. It has only one form and it rests on the writing line.

When the *alif* is joined to its right, it is written as a vertical stroke from the bottom up. The *alif* represents the long vowel *aa*. It can also represent the short vowels *a, i,* or *u,* which depends on its vocalisation (see pages 48 and 52).

baa', taa', and thaa'

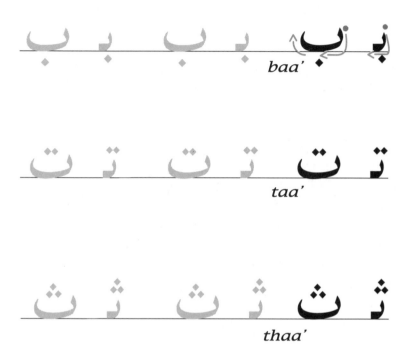

baa'

taa'

thaa'

The *baa'*, *taa'*, and *thaa'* are all joined letters and each has two forms. The short form of the letter is used at the beginning of a word or between two other joined letters. The full form is written when the letter falls at the end of a word or when it stands alone.

The dot under the *baa'* is an integral part of the letter and must not be omitted. Similarly, the two dots on the *taa'* and the three dots on the *thaa'* must be kept.

a father *abb*

door *baab*

daddy *ba'ba*

to broadcast *bath*

steadiness *thabaat*

9

geem, Haa', and khaa'

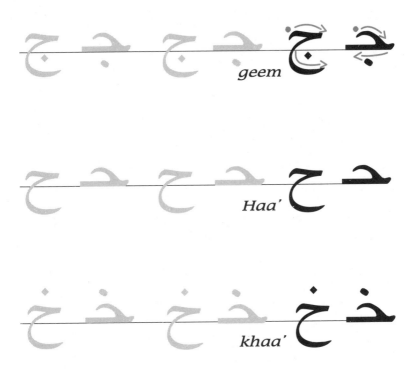

geem

Haa'

khaa'

These three letters belong to the category of joined letters. They each have a short and long form and their shape changes according to their position in a word. The geem (also known as jiim) has a dot underneath, the Haa' has no dots, and the khaa' has one dot on top.

The short form rests on the writing line. The full form starts above the line and then curls beneath it.

حُبّ

love **Hub**

اِخْت

sister **'ukht**

بَحْث

research **baHth**

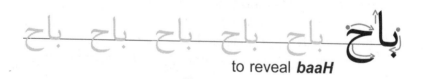

بَاح

to reveal **baaH**

تَحْت

under/below **taHat**

Notes and Review:
First Set of Letters

℃ The letters *baa'* (ب), *taa'* (ت) and *thaa'* (ث) are easy to pronounce. The *baa'* is similar to the English letter *b*, as in the word "boy." Note that in the Arabic language there is no equivalent to the letter *p*, so the *baa'* is always used to transliterate the *p*.

℃ The *taa'* has a familiar sound, much like the English letter *t* as in "toy."

℃ The *thaa'* has no direct equivalent in English. Its sound is similar to the letters *th* as in "theatre."

℃ The *geem* (ج) has two possible pronunciations, which depend on the specific dialect used. In Egyptian Arabic, for example, it is pronounced *g* as in "gap." Most other dialects pronounce it more like a *j* as in "John."

℃ The *Haa'* (ح) is difficult to learn because it has no direct equivalent in English. The closest sound is the English letter *h*. The *Haa'*, however, has a more emphatic and heavy sound than the *h* (see page 42). When we refer to the *Haa'*, we will capitalise it to indicate the emphatic sound it produces.

℃ The *khaa'* (خ) sounds like the letters *kh* as in "Khan" or *ch* as in "Bach."

خث حث حث حث حث حث حث

to urge/incite **Hath**

تاج تاج تاج تاج تاج تاج تاج

crown **taag**

حج حج حج حج حج حج حج

pilgrimage **Hag**

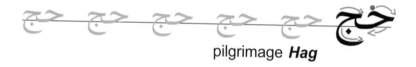

بخت بخت بخت بخت بخت بخت

luck **bakhet**

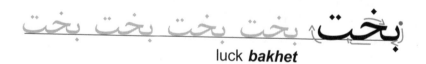

باحث باحث باحث باحث باحث

researcher **baaHeth**

13

daal and dhaal

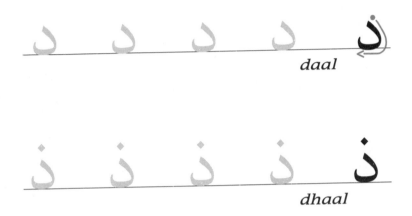

daal

dhaal

The *daal* and *dhaal* are both disjoined letters. They do not join the letter that follows, and their shape does not change according to their position in a word. They have only one form each, and they both rest on the writing line. The *dhaal* has one dot on top, while the *daal* has none.

The *daal* is equivalent to the English letter *d* as in "dad." The *dhaal* has no direct equivalent in English. The closest sound is the letters *th* as in "this" or as in "with." The *dhaal* is usually transliterated as *dh*.

دب دب دب دب دب دب دب

a bear *deb*

جد جد جد جد جد جد جد

grandfather *gid*

بجد بجد بجد بجد بجد بجد

seriously *begad*

جذب جذب جذب جذب جذب جذب

to attract *gadhab*

ذباب ذباب ذباب ذباب ذباب ذباب

flies (insect) *dhubaab*

raa' and zaay

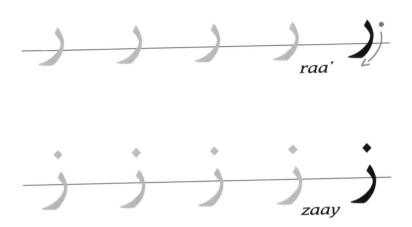

raa'

zaay

The *raa'* and *zaay* (also known as *zayn*) belong to the family of disjoined letters and have only one form each. Both letters share the same basic shape. The *zaay*, however, has a dot on top while the *raa'* has none. Each letter starts above the writing line and then curves below it. Note that approximately one third of the letter appears above the line and two thirds beneath it.

The sound of the letter *raa'* is similar to the English letter *r* as in "Rome." The *zaay* is equivalent to the letter *z* as is "zoo."

أرز ارز ارز ارز ارز ارز ارز

rice *urz*

حر حر حر حر حر حر حر

hot (weather) *Harr*

برد برد برد برد برد برد برد

cold *bard*

جار جار جار جار جار جار جار

neighbour *gaar*

زبد زبد زبد زبد زبد زبد

butter *zibd*

seen and sheen

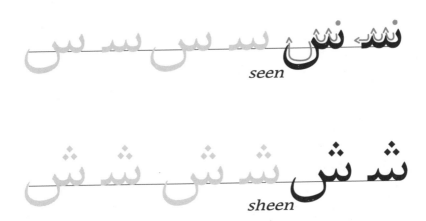

seen

sheen

The *seen* and *sheen* belong to the family of joined letters. They each have a short and a long form. The two letters share the same shape except that the *sheen* has three dots arranged as a triangle on top.

The short form rests on the writing line. The long form starts on the line and then descends underneath it, forming a semicircle.

The letter *seen* is equivalent to the English letter *s.* The *sheen* sounds like the letters *sh* as in "she."

أُسْتَاذ استاذ استاذ استاذ استاذ

mister/professor **ustaaz**

جَرَس جرس جرس جرس جرس

bell **garas**

أَسَاس اساس اساس اساس اساس

foundation **'asaas**

شَبَاب شباب شباب شباب شباب

youth **shabaab**

خَدَش خدش خدش خدش خدش

to scratch **khadsh**

19

Saad and Daad

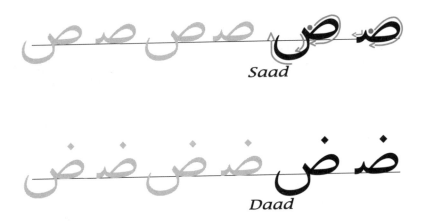

Saad

Daad

These two letters have no direct equivalent in English. *The Saad* sounds like a heavy *s.* Try pronouncing the word "sun" while stressing the *s.* The *Daad* also has no equivalent in English. The closest pronunciation to the letter *Daad* is the sound of a stressed *d* as in the English word "dome."

Both letters belong to the family of joined letters and they have two forms each. The short form of the letter rests on the writing line. The long form starts on the line, curves underneath it, and then comes up again to rest just above the line. Take special note of the upward stroke in the short form of both letters.

صباح

morning *SabaaH*

حصد

to harvest *HaSad*

خاص

private *khaaS*

ضباب

fog *Dabaab*

أرض

land *aarD*

21

Taa' and Zaa'

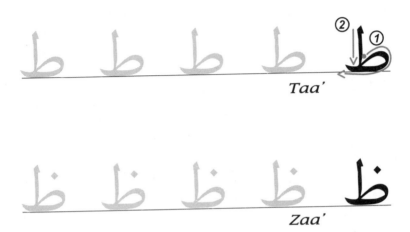

Taa'

Zaa'

Taa' and *Zaa'* belong to the family of joined letters. However, they have only one form each and their shape does not change according to their position in a word. They rest on the writing line. To write the letters, start with the bottom part first and add the stroke. Then, add a dot on the Zaa'

Neither of these letters has a direct equivalent in English. The *Taa'* sounds like a bold or stressed *t*. The *Zaa'* (which has one dot) sounds like a stressed *z*.

طباخ

cook *Tabaakh*

خطأ

mistake/error *khaTaa'*

بط

duck *baT*

حظ

luck *HaZ*

ضابط

officer *DaabbiT*

Notes and Review:
Second Set of Letters

You have been introduced to four new letters whose sounds are unfamiliar to non-Arabic speakers: *Saad* (ص), *Daad* (ض), *Taa'* (ط), and *Zaa'* (ظ). However, they are not hard to master. These letters do have familiar equivalents in English, but they need to be pronounced much more forcefully and in a deeper tone. In this book, we will capitalise all references to these letters to indicate the emphatic sound they produce.

Pay careful attention that you distinguish the sounds of these letters from similar letters learned previously. The similar couples are as follows:

☾ The *Saad* (ص) and the *seen* (س): The *seen* sounds like the English letter *s*, while the *Saad* sounds like a deep and bold *s*

☾ The *Daad* (ض) and the *daal* (د): The *daal* is equivalent to the English letter *d,* while the *Daad* is a more forceful and bolder *d*.

☾ The *Taa'* (ط) and the *taa'* (ت): The letter *Taa'* is a bold strong *t*. The letter *taa'* is the direct equivalent to the letter *t*.

☾ Finally, do not mistake the sound of the *Zaa'* (ظ) for the *zaay* (ز). The *Zaa'* is a strong bold *z*, while the *zaay* is the direct equivalent to the English letter *z*.

24

صبر صبر صبر صبر صبر **صبر**
patience *Sabr*

ستر ستر ستر ستر ستر **ستر**
to hide/conceal *satr*

سطر سطر سطر سطر سطر **سطر**
line *saTr*

درس درس درس درس **درس**
lesson *dars*

ضرس ضرس ضرس ضرس **ضرس**
tooth *Ders*

25

'ayn

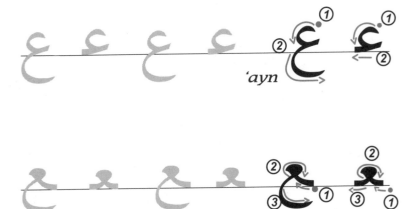

'ayn

The 'ayn is difficult to learn. It is a joined letter and has four different shapes. The first, reading from right to left, appears at the beginning of a word and rests on the writing line.

The second shape is used when the 'ayn is standing alone, or at the end of a word after a disjoined letter. It begins just above the line and continues underneath.

The third form of the 'ayn falls in the middle of a word between two joined letters. The last example, shows the 'ayn when it falls at the end of a word after a joined letter. It begins on top of the line and then curves below it.

عيش عيش عيش عيش عيش **عيش**

bread *ᶜeysh*

شارع شارع شارع شارع **شارع**

street *sharaᶜ*

صعب صعب صعب صعب **صعب**

difficult *saᶜb*

طبعاً طبعاً طبعاً طبعاً **طبعاً**

of course *Tabaᶜan*

ربع ربع ربع ربع ربع **ربع**

quarter *robaᶜ*

ghayn

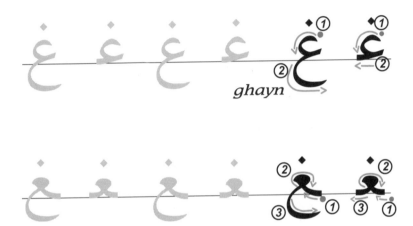

ghayn

The *ghayn* is similar in shape to the letter *'ayn*; the only difference is that the *ghayn* has a dot on top while the *'ayn* has none.

The *'ayn* and *ghayn* have no direct equivalent in English. Their sounds are not familiar to most non-Arabic speakers. You need to listen carefully to their pronunciation and try to practice the sound. The *ghayn* is transliterated as *gh*, while the *'ayn* is usually transcribed as ᶜ indicating that this sound is unique and there is no match in the English alphabet. If you still find it hard to master the sound of the *'ayn*, try to think of it as an emphatic or long *a*, as in Verdi's opera "Aida." This is not really accurate, but it will be the closest sound it imitates. The closest sound for the *ghayn* are the letters *gh* in "Baghdad."

غراب غراب غراب غراب غراب

raven **ghorab**

غرب غرب غرب غرب غرب

west **gharb**

غداً غداً غداً غداً غداً

tomorrow **ghadan**

بغداد بغداد بغداد بغداد بغداد

Baghdad

تبغ تبغ تبغ تبغ تبغ

tobacco **tabgh**

29

faa' and qaaf

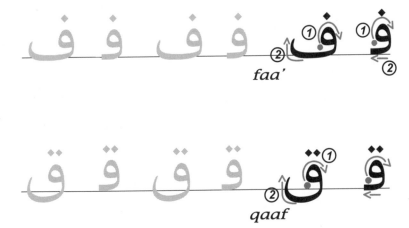

faa'

qaaf

The *faa'* and *qaaf* share the same short form, but their long forms are different. Their short forms rest on the writing line. The *faa'* has one dot while the *qaaf* has two. The long form of the *faa'* is elongated and rests on the line, whereas that of the *qaaf* starts just above the line and then descends beneath it forming half a circle.

Faa' is similar to the English letter *f*. The *qaaf* has no direct equivalent; the closest you can find to its sound is the letter *q* as in "Iraq."

فقد فقد فقد فقد فقد

to lose *faqad*

تفاح تفاح تفاح تفاح تفاح

apples *tufaaH*

قطف قطف قطف قطف

to pick (flowers) *qaTaf*

قطار قطار قطار قطار قطار

train *qeTaar*

شرق شرق شرق شرق شرق

east *sharq*

kaaf

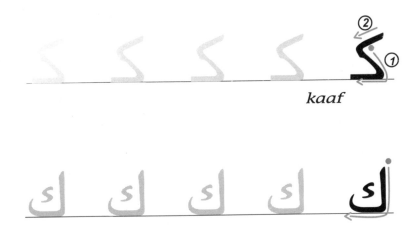

kaaf

Kaaf is a joined letter, and has two forms. The short form is used in the beginning or middle of a word. To write the *kaaf,* start with the base of the letter and then add the top stroke.

The full form occurs when the letter stands alone or at the end of a word. The full form rests on the writing line. What's inside the *kaaf* is a *hamza,* (see page 48). It is an integral part of the letter, but has no effect on its pronunciation.

The letter *kaaf* is similar in its pronunciation to the English letter *k*.

كتاب كتاب كتاب كتاب كتاب

book *kitaab*

سكر سكر سكر سكر سكر

sugar *sukar*

شكراً شكراً شكراً شكراً شكراً

thank you *shukraan*

كشك كشك كشك كشك كشك

kiosk *kushek*

شباك شباك شباك شباك شباك

window *shubbaak*

33

laam

laam

The *laam* is similar to the English letter *l*. It is a joined letter and has two forms. The short form rests on the writing line. The full form starts above the line; its tail descends below the line and then curves up again just above it.

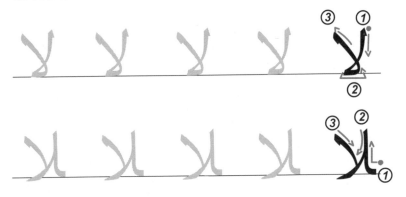

The *laam* and the *alif* have a unique shape when they are joined together. The first example shows the two letters when standing alone. The second shape is used when the *laam* is joined from its right; it then connects with the *alif* to form this distinctive shape. Remember that the *alif* is a disjoined letter, meaning it never joins the letter following it.

لتر لتر لتر لتر لتر لتر أَلْتر

liter *letr*

كلب كلب كلب كلب كلب كَلب

dog *kaleb*

الف الف الف الف الف الِف

thousand *alf*

فلفل فلفل فلفل فلفل فلفل فَلْفَل

pepper *felfel*

تلال تلال تلال تلال تلال تِلال

hills *telaal*

Notes and Review:
The Prefix alif laam

At this point, let us pause to discuss the definite article "the."

In Arabic there is no equivalent to the English "the." The prefix *alif laam* (الـ) serves instead as the definite article. It is also worth noting that in Arabic an adjective has to agree with a noun; if the noun is masculine or feminine, definite or indefinite, singular or plural, the adjective must follow the same form.

In the last two examples (on the facing page) you will notice that since the *alif laam* prefix indicates that the noun is definite, its adjective must have the prefix agree as well.

You will find the definite article used more frequently in Arabic than in English, especially in general terms and in expressions like love, life, or patience. For example, "life is beautiful" becomes "the life is beautiful."

There are no indefinite articles such as "a" and "an" in the Arabic language, you simply leave them out.

الصبر

patience **el-saber**

الرجل

the man **el-ragoul**

الاخبار

the news **el-akhbaar**

الدور الرابع

the fourth floor **el-door el-raba**[c]

البرد القارس

the bitter cold **el-bard el-qaress**

meem

meem

The letter *meem* corresponds to the English letter *m* as in "moon." It is a joined letter with two forms. The short form rests on the writing line, while the full form begins on the line and then descends underneath it.

When the final *meem* is joined to another letter, it is usually written as a circle counter-clockwise. After completing the circle, you add the tail.

ملك ملك ملك ملك ملك **ملك**

king *malek*

مطار مطار مطار مطار **مطار**

airport *maTaar*

قمر قمر قمر قمر **قمر**

moon *qamar*

تمام تمام تمام تمام **تمام**

perfect *tamaam*

مطعم مطعم مطعم مطعم **مطعم**

restaurant *maTᶜam*

39

noon

noon

The *noon* is a joined letter with two forms. The short form rests on the writing line and is similar in shape to the letters *baa'* (ب), *taa'* (ت), and *thaa'* (ث), which you studied earlier. The long form is different. It is round, resembling half a circle, and begins above the line and then curls underneath it.

The *noon* has only one dot, positioned as shown above. The dot is an integral part of the letter. Remember, it is always best to write the basic part of the letter first, and then add any additional dots or strokes. The *noon* is similar in its pronunciation to the English letter *n* as in "near."

fire *naar*

bank *bank*

milk *laban*

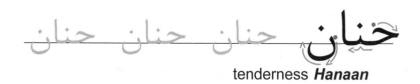

tenderness *Hanaan*

فنجان

cup *fingaan*

haa'

haa'

The *haa'* has four shapes. Reading from right to left, you notice the first form, when the *haa'* falls at the beginning of a word. The second form—the egg-shaped *haa'*—illustrates the letter when standing alone or at the end of a word after a disjoined letter. The third form occurs when the *haa'* falls between two joined letters, and the last shape, when the *haa'* falls at the end of a word after a joined letter.

The *haa'* is pronounced like the English letter *h*. Many students of the Arabic language confuse the sounds of the *haa'* and the *Haa'* (ح). The latter (see page 10) has no equivalent in English, but sounds like a heavily accented *h*.

هرم

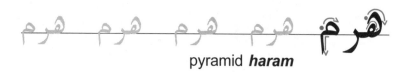

pyramid *haram*

هدهد

hoopoe (type of bird) *hodhod*

إنتباه

attention *intebaah*

شهر

month *shahr*

جنيه

pound (currency) *gineeh*

43

waaw

waaw

The *waaw* is similar in pronunciation to the English letter *w*. It can also represent the long vowel *oo*. The letter starts with a circle written clockwise, which starts and ends on the line. The tail of the letter descends in a slight curve beneath the writing line. The *waaw* is another disjoined letter and has only one form.

Remember, a disjoined letter joins the letter to its right, but **does not join** the letter that follows it. Disjoined letters have only one shape, as their form does not change according to their position in a word. The six disjoined letters are the *alif* (ﺍ), *daal* (ﺩ), *dhaal* (ﺫ), *raa'* (ﺭ), *zaay* (ﺯ), and *waaw* (ﻭ).

ورق ورق ورق ورق ورق

paper *waraq*

لون لون لون لون لون

colour *lown*

صوت صوت صوت صوت

voice/sound *Sout*

ورد ورد ورد ورد ورد

flowers *ward*

وصول وصول وصول وصول وصول

arrival *weSool*

45

yaa'

yaa'

The *yaa'* has two forms. The short form should by now look familiar to you. This time it rests on the writing line with two dots underneath. The full form is unique. It starts above the line, curves beneath it, and then up again. Remember, the short form of the letter is used at the beginning of a word, or when it falls between two other joined letters. The full form appears when the letter is standing alone or at the end of a word.

The *yaa'* is similar to the English letter *y*. It can also represent the sound of the long vowel *ee*.

يوم يوم يوم يوم يوم **يوم**

day *yoom*

يمين يمين يمين يمين **يمين**

right *yemeen*

شاى شاى شاى شاى **شاى**

tea *shaay*

تاكسى تاكسى تاكسى تاكسى **تاكسى**

taxi *taxi*

حبيبى حبيبى حبيبى حبيبى **حبيبى**

my love *Habeebi*

hamza

hamza

The *hamza* has no specific sound. It indicates a glottal stop. It is usually transcribed as an apostrophe and it indicates a vocal break. The *hamza* is usually carried by the *alif*, the *waaw*, or the *yaa'*. It can also occur alone at the end of a word; in this case the *hamza* is placed on the writing line.

The *hamza* and the *alif* have a unique relationship together. The *hamza* can occur above or under the *alif*. When the *hamza* occurs above the letter, (أ) the *alif* is pronounced as an *a*. When the *hamza* occurs underneath, the *alif* (إ) is pronounced as an *i*.

48

أنباء

news *anbaa'*

إملاء

dictation *imlaa'*

سؤال

question *su'oaal*

رئيس

president *ra'ees*

شئ

thing *shee'*

49

taa' marbouta

taa' marbouta

The *taa' marbouta* is not an alphabet letter; it is more of a feminine mark. In Arabic, all nouns are either masculine or feminine. Most, although not all, feminine nouns end with the *taa' marbouta*. A masculine noun can end in any letter. Remember that a noun and an adjective have to agree, so if a noun is feminine, its adjective will also end with the same feminine mark.

For example:

Happy family	ᶜa'yla sᶜeeda	عائلة سعيدة
Pretty woman	imra'a gameela	إمرأة جميلة

The *taa' marbouta* is found only at the end of a word. It has two forms that are a variation of the letter *haa'* (see page 42). The egg shape with two dots is used when the *taa' marbouta* falls at the end of a word after a disjoined letter. The second shape is used when it falls at the end of a word after a joined letter. The *taa' marbouta* is commonly pronounced as an *a*.

دكتور

doctor *duktoor*

دكتورة

doctor (female) *duktoora*

جميلة

pretty *gameela*

قهوة

coffee *qahwa*

هدية

gift *hedeeya*

Vowel marks

Arabic has three special vowel marks, which are not letters of the alphabet. The first vowel mark is the *kasra* ( ). It is written below the consonant it vocalises and represents the short vowel *i* as in "pit." The second vowel mark, *fatHaa* ( ), is written above the letter and represents the vowel *a* like in "sat". The third, the *dama* ( ), is written above the letter and represents the short vowel *u* as in "up."

Example:

baa' and a *kasra*　　بِ　　is pronounced bi

baa' and *fatHaa*　　بَ　　is pronounced ba

baa' and a *dama*　　بُ　　is pronounced bu

The pronunciation of a word, and therefore its meaning, can change according to its vocalisation. This is demonstrated in the examples on the facing page.

There are two additional marks to discuss, which are not vowel marks but do affect the way a word is pronounced. The first is the *shadda* ( ). When the *shadda* occurs above a consonant, the consonant is pronounced as a doubled letter. The other is the *tanween* mark, which resembles two *fatHaas* stacked one on the other ( ). The t*anween* sounds like an *n* and usually appears over the *alif*. It can only be placed at the end of a word (see the example *shukraan* on page 33).

كَتَبَ كَتَبَ كَتَبَ كَتَبَ كَتَبَ **كَتَبَ**

to write *kataba*

كُتُب كُتُب كُتُب كُتُب كُتُب **كُتُب**

books *kotoub*

مَدرسَة مَدرسَة مَدرسَة **مَدرسَة**

school *madrasa*

مُدرِّسَة مُدرِّسَة مُدرِّسَة **مُدرِّسَة**

teacher (female) *modarresa*

شبَّاك شبَّاك شبَّاك شبَّاك **شبَّاك**

window *shubbak*

Numbers

The number system we use in English was developed from the Arabic more than 500 years ago, and is today commonly known as the Arabic numeral system. Over the years, however, numbers in both parts of the world evolved in different ways. For our purposes, we will refer to numbers used in English as "European numerals" and those used in the Arabic language as "Arabic numerals."

As both systems share the same origin, there are a number of similarities between Arabic and European numerals. Most importantly, numbers composed in Arabic are written from left to right, exactly as in English. So, when you combine words and numbers, you read the word from right to left, but the number from left to right.

Example: **House No. 6702**

Translates to: بيت رقم : ٦٧٠٢

℃ Pay careful attention to the zero (◆), which resembles a dot, and the five (٥), which resembles a zero in European numerals.

℃ In North African countries, European numerals are used in place of Arabic ones, which means that the previous example reads: **6702** :بيت رقم

℃ Today, with new Web technologies, you will find many Arabic Web sites using European numerals instead of Arabic ones.

٣‌ ٢ ١   ٣‌ ٢ ١   ٣‌ ٢ ١   ٣‌ ٢ ١

3 2 1

٦ ٥ ٤   ٦ ٥ ٤   ٦ ٥ ٤   ٦ ٥ ٤

6 5 4

٩ ٨ ٧   ٩ ٨ ٧   ٩ ٨ ٧   ٩ ٨ ٧

9 8 7

١٢ ١١ ١٠   ١٢ ١١ ١٠   ١٢ ١١ ١٠

12 11 10

٢٢ ٢١ ٢٠   ٢٢ ٢١ ٢٠   ٢٢ ٢١ ٢٠

22 21 20

٥٠ ٤٠ ٣٠   ٥٠ ٤٠ ٣٠   ٥٠ ٤٠ ٣٠

50 40 30

٦٥   ٦٥   ٦٥   ٦٥   ٦٥   **٦٥**

65

١٧٠   ١٧٠   ١٧٠   ١٧٠   ١٧٠   **١٧٠**

170

٦٨٠٣   ٦٨٠٣   ٦٨٠٣   **٦٨٠٣**

6803

٢٤٥٦٨   ٢٤٥٦٨   **٢٤٥٦٨**

24568

٣٩١٠٦٤٥٧   **٣٩١٠٦٤٥٧**

39106457

الساعة ١٢ الساعة ١٢ الساعة ١٢

12 o'clock   *el saaᶜa itnasher*

٤٥٠ مدعو ٤٥٠ مدعو ٤٥٠ مدعو

450 guests   *roboᶜumya wa khamseen madᶜoo*

شارع٣٠٨ شارع٣٠٨ شارع٣٠٨

street 308   *sharaᶜ tholthomeea wa thamania*

١٦٠ دولار ١٦٠ دولار ١٦٠ دولار

160 dollars   *meea wa seteyn dollar*

صفحة ٧٩ صفحة ٧٩ صفحة ٧٩

page 79   *safHaa tesaᶜ wa sabᶜeyn*

Handwriting

ح حـ جـج ثـ ثـ تـ تـ بـ ب ا

شـ شـ سـ سـ ز ر ذ د خـ خـ

غـ غـ عـ عـ ظ ط ضـ ضـ صـ صـ

نـ نـ مـ م لـ كـ كـ قـ قـ فـ ف

ىـ ىـ يـ و هـ ه

١ ٢ ٣ ٤ ٥ ٦ ٧ ٨ ٩ ١٠

Until now, we have concentrated on the printed version of the Arabic alphabet. There are only a few differences between printed and handwritten Arabic. The next few pages will guide you through handwritten script. It is recommended, however, that you learn the classic or printed form of writing first, since you can't go wrong with printing. As your comfort level with the alphabet progresses, you will be able to develop your own writing style.

Notes on Handwriting

☾ When a letter has more than one dot on top or bottom, the dots are usually joined together. For example, the two dots under the *yaa'* (‎ـﻲ) join to form a dash, and the three dots on top of the *thaa'* (‎ﺛ) form a triangle.

☾ In handwritten Arabic, the *seen* (‎ﺳ) and the *sheen* (‎ﺷ) lose their sharp upward points and are written as a flat line.

☾ Letters that end with a dot, such as the *noon*, *Daad*, *qaaf*, and *sheen,* are sometimes written with an outside stroke in place of the dot (‎ ‎ ‎ ‎).

☾ The final *noon* can be written in two different ways. The dot can be replaced by an outside stroke or it can coil inside the letter (‎ ‎).

☾ When writing the *kaaf*, a curl can sometimes be placed inside it, instead of the *hamza* (‎ﻚ).

☾ The middle *haa'* is handwritten as (‎) and the final form can be written as: ‎ . Similarly, the *taa' marbouta* will be written as: ‎ .

☾ In numbers, the upward point of number two is flattened out (‎), and number three (‎) loses one of its points. Note that three in handwriting resembles two in print; try not to confuse between them.

59

شرق

East **sharq**

ثلج

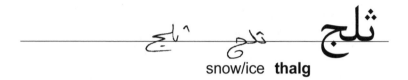

snow/ice **thalg**

قماش

cloth **qumaash**

نهر

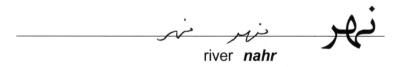

river **nahr**

ارض

land **arD**

مستشفى
hospital *mustashfa*

مشكلة
problem *mushkela*

تأمين
insurance *ta'meen*

جمرك
customs *gumruk*

فندق
hotel *funduq*

Part Two

Exercises

Exercise 1

In this exercise, you are given the short form of the letter. Write the long form. The first one has been done for you. Be sure to practice a few times.

ح- F	ت ت ت ت ت ت -A
ش- G	ق -B
ل -H	غ -C
ف -I	ک -D
ئ -J	م -E

Exercise 2

In this exercise, you are given the long form of the letter.
Write the short form. Practice a few times.

ك -A _____   س -F _____

ض -B _____   ى -G _____

ث -C _____   م -H _____

خ -D _____   ق -I _____

ظ -E _____   ع -J _____

Exercise 3

Write the missing letters in the squares provided. The first exercise is done for you.

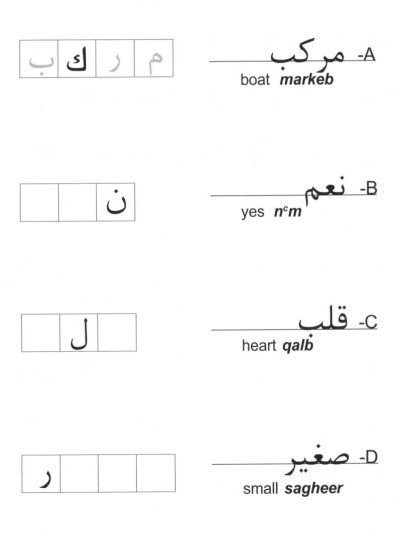

A-‎مركب‎
boat ***markeb***

B-‎نعم‎
yes ***n^{c}m***

C-‎قلب‎
heart ***qalb***

D-‎صغير‎
small ***sagheer***

	ب	

E -جبل _____
mountain *gabel*

ف		

F -صيف _____
summer *Saeef*

		ر

G -ربيع _____
spring *rabee*[c]

	ا	

H -شتاء _____
winter *shetaa'*

		خ

I -خريف _____
autumn *khareef*

Exercise 4

In this exercise, you are given the words in handwritten script. Write the letters in the squares provided. The first word is done for you.

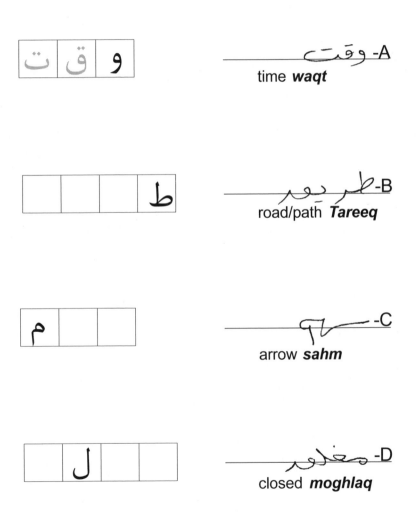

و	ق	تَ

A- وقَتَ
time **waqt**

			ط

B- طَريق
road/path **Tareeq**

		م

C- سهم
arrow **sahm**

	ل		

D- مغلق
closed **moghlaq**

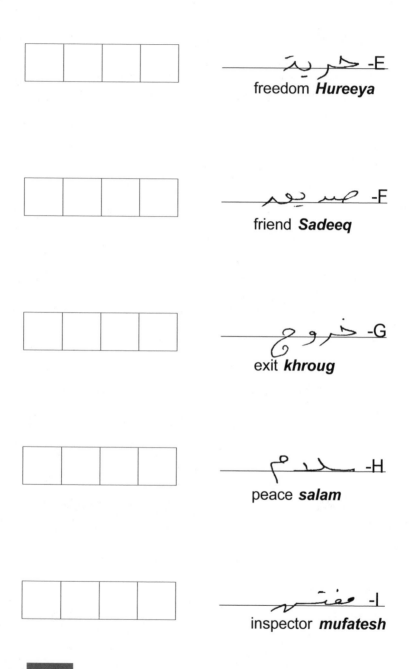

‫حرية‬ -E
freedom **Hureeya**

‫صديق‬ -F
friend **Sadeeq**

‫خروج‬ -G
exit **khroug**

‫سلام‬ -H
peace **salam**

‫مفتش‬ -I
inspector **mufatesh**

Exercise 5

Match each profession to its Arabic equivalent. Use the transliteration as a guide. The first exercise is done for you.

i- Farmer _____
   falaaH

A-صحفى

ii- Engineer _____
   muhandis

B-فلاح

iii- Journalist _____
   SaHafee

C-محامى

iv- Teacher _____
   mudaris

D-مهندس

v- Lawyer _____
   muHaamy

E-مدرس

vi-Manager (female)
mudeera
F-سائق

vii- Driver
sa'aek
G-مديرة

viii- Consultant
mustashaar
H-صيدلى

ix-Employee (female)
muwaZafa
ا-ممرضة

x-Nurse(female)
mumareDa
ل-موظفة

xi- Pharmacist
Saydalee
ك-مستشار

Exercise 6

Rearrange these Arab countries according to their alphabetical order.

A- مصر _____

Egypt

F- ليبيا _____

Libya

B- الاردن _____

Jordan

G- اليمن _____

Yemen

C- سوريا _____

Syria

H- لبنان _____

Lebanon

D- المغرب _____

Morocco

I- تونس _____

Tunisia

E- قطر _____

Qatar

J- البحرين _____

Bahrain

Exercise 7

Rearrange these Arab capitals according to their alphabetical order.

عمان -F
_____
Amman

طرابلس -A
_____
Tripoli

بغداد -G
_____
Baghdad

الرياض -B
_____
Riyadh

الرباط -H
_____
Rabat

صنعاء -C
_____
Sana'a

ابوظبى -I
_____
Abu Dhabi

بيروت -D
_____
Beirut

دمشق -J
_____
Damascus

الخرطوم -E
_____
Khartoum

Exercise 8

Match each Arabic number to its English equivalent.

i- 565   ١٢ -A

ii- 91   ١٩ -B

iii- 060   ٥٦٥ -C

iv- 19   ٩١ -D

v- 12   ٠٦٠ -E

Exercise 9

Match each of the following house and street numbers to its English equivalent.

i- House 985 _____   ‏A- شارع رقم ٨٥٠٦‏

ii- Street 6058 _____   ‏B- بيت رقم ٥٨٩‏

iii- Street 8056 _____   ‏C- شارع رقم ٨٠٥٦‏

iv- Street 8506 _____   ‏D- شارع رقم ٦٠٥٨‏

v- House 589 _____   ‏E- بيت رقم ٩٨٥‏

75

Exercise 10

Solve these simple equations. Remember, answers must be in Arabic.

$\underline{\hspace{3cm}} = ١٦ + ٢٤$ -F $\underline{\hspace{3cm}} = ٢٠ \times ٤$ -A

$\underline{\hspace{3cm}} = ٧ \div ٢٨$ -G $\underline{\hspace{3cm}} = ١٠٠ - ٣٠٠$ -B

$\underline{\hspace{3cm}} = ٥٥ - ١٥٠$ -H $\underline{\hspace{3cm}} = ٤٥ + ٢٥$ -C

$\underline{\hspace{3cm}} = ٣ \div ٦٦$ -I $\underline{\hspace{3cm}} = ١٢ \times ٨$ -D

$\underline{\hspace{3cm}} = ٥ \times ٧$ -J $\underline{\hspace{3cm}} = ١٠ \div ٢٠$ -E

Exercise 11

Match each Arabic date, price, and quantity to its English equivalent.

i- 893/4 kilos   ٢٠٠٣/٧/١٨ -A

ii- 505 liras   ٥١٫٢٥ دولار -B

iii- 5.5 liras   ١٩٨١/٧/٣٠ -C

iv- 51.25 dollars   ٨٩٫٣/٤ كيلو -D

v- 25.51 dollars   ٥٠٥ ليرة -E

vi- 18/7/2003   ٥٫٥ ليرة -F

vii- 30/7/1981   ٢٥٫٥١ دولار -G

Exercise 12

Join the letters together to form a word. The first exercise is done for you.

A- ب ی ت بيت _____
house/home *beyt*

B- س و ق _____
market *souq*

C- س ه م _____
arrow *sahm*

D- ن و ر _____
light *noor*

E- خ ط ر _____
danger *khaTar*

F- عوننمم

forbidden **mamnoo**[c]

G- ةعماج

university **gamaᶜa**

H- رىغص

small **Sagheer**

I- القاهرة

Cairo **el-qahera**

J- أوتوبىس

bus **utoobees**

K- ج ب ل
mountain *gabal*

L- ح ف ل ة
party *Hafla*

M- س ك و ت
silence *sekoot*

N- ص ح ر ا ء
desert *Sahraa'*

O- ص د ى ق
friend *Sadeeq*

P- ك ل ا م

talk *kalaam*

Q- ع ا ئ ل ة

family *ᶜa'yla*

R- م غ ل ق

closed *mughlaq*

S- م ش ك ل ة

problem *mushkela*

T- ف ا ك ه ة

fruit *faakeha*

Exercise 13

Match each noun with an adjective. You are given the translation of the noun followed by the required adjective combination. However, of the three adjectives next to each noun, only one is correct.

سعيد سعيدة السعيد	A- يوم Day (*good day*)
البعيدة بعيد البعيد	B- البحر Sea (*the far sea*)
العالى عالى عالية	C- جبل Mountain (*a high mountain*)
شقية شقى الشقى	D- طفلة Child (*naughty child*)

E- بيت
House
(an old house)

قديمة
القديم
قديم

F- المديرة
Manager
(the new manager)

الجديد
جديدة
الجديدة

G- حجرة
Room
(a clean room)

النظيفة
نظيفة
لانظيفة

H- الدور
Floor
(the second floor)

الثانى
الثانية
ثانى

Exercise 14

Make each adjective either definite or feminine according
to the noun provided. The first example is done for you

A- البحر (احمر)

البحر الاحمر

The Red Sea

B- المطعم (غالى)

_____

The expensive restaurant

C- الرجل (لطيف)

_____

The nice man

D- القهوة (ساخن)

_____

The hot coffee

E- إمرأة (لطيف)

_____

A nice woman

F- الشارع (ضيق)

_____

The narrow street

G- الأخ (غنى)

_____

The rich brother

H- الحجرة (مغلق)

_____

The closed room

I- تذكرة (رخيص)

_____

A cheap ticket

J- العصير (طازج)

_____

The fresh juice

K- الصديق (وفى)

_____

The loyal friend

Exercise 15

There is a four-letter word hidden in this puzzle. Can you find it?

Find and cross out each of the words listed on the facing page. Cross out the words vertically, horizontally, or diagonally. When you're done, you'll be left with the hidden word.

م	د	ج	ش	س	ر	د
ح	ع	ل	ا	خ	ا	م
ل	ب	ب	ر	ر	ر	ك
م	ا	ن	ع	ح	ى	ا
م	و	ى	ب	م	ع	ت
ف	ق	أ	ت	ح	ت	ب
ر	ح	ب	أ	ل	ه	ا

اهلاً

hello **ahlan**

ام

mother **um**

اخ

brother **akh**

جد

grandfather **ged**

تحت

underneath **taHt**

بحر

sea **baHr**

عم

uncle **ᶜm**

شارع

street **shaarᶜ**

درس

lesson **darss**

لبن

milk **laban**

كاتب

kaateb **writer**

قف

stop **qef**

يوم

day **yoom**

محل

store **maHal**

مرحباً

welcome **marHaban**

Writing Exercises

Below are a number of exercises for you to practice your writing. Remember to position the letter correctly either above or underneath the line. Don't forget to place the dots in their right places.

أُستاذ
_____

master/teacher

إمرأة
_____

woman

برج
_____

tower

بعيد
_____

far away

توائم
twins

ثمن
price

جرس
bell

حرية
freedom

حصان
horse

خروف
lamb

خطأ
error/mistake

دليل
guide

دافئ
warm

ذئب
wolf

رياح
wind

زهرة
flower

سيارة
car

شتاء
winter

شرطة
police

صيدلية

pharmacy

ضريبة

tax

ضيف

guest

طائرة

airplane

طبيب

doctor

ظلام

darkness

عروسة

doll/bride

عنوان

address

غرفة

room

غيور

jealous

فائز

winner

قصة

story

قاضى

judge

كثير

much/many

كوبرى

bridge

لغة

language

ليل

night

مدينة

city

موسيقى

music

نجوم

stars

هدوء

quietness

هدية

gift

ولاء

loyalty

يسار

left

يمين

right

واحد
one

إثنين
two

ثلاثة
three

أربعة
four

خمسة
five

ستة
six

سبعة
seven

ثمانية
eight

تسعة
nine

عشرة
ten

يوم
day

أسبوع
week

شهر
month

الأحد
Sunday

الاثنين
Monday

الثلاثاء
Tuesday

الأربعاء
Wednesday

الخميس
Thursday

الجمعة
Friday

السبت
Saturday

مرحباً

hello

اهلاً وسهلاً

hello & welcome

صباح الخير

good morning

السلام عليكم

peace be upon you
(a traditional greeting)

وعليكم السلام

and peace be upon
you (reply)

101

كيف حالك؟

how are you?

أنا بخير

I am fine

كم الساعة؟

what is the time?

العاشرة والربع

quarter past ten

شكراً

thank you

من فضلك
please

الحمدلله
thank God

إن شاء الله
God willing

ما إسمك؟
what is your name?

أنا إسمى ---
my name is ---

103

ما عمرك؟

how old are you?

ماذا تعمل؟

what do you do?

أين تقيم؟

where do you live?

من أين أنت؟

where are you from?

هل تعرف العربية؟

do you know Arabic?

أين الفندق؟
where is the hotel?

أريد خريطة
I want a map

احتاج مساعدة
I need help

مع السلامة
good bye

إلى اللقاء
until we meet again

Answers

Exercise 1

B-ق C-غ D-ك E-م F-ح G-ش H-ل ا-ف J-ئ

Exercise 2

A-ك B-ض C-ث D-خ E-ظ F-س G-ر H-م ا-ق J-ع

Exercise 3

B-نعم C-قلب D-صغیر E-جبل F-صیف
G-ربیع H-شتاء ا-خریف

Exercise 4

B-طریق C-سهم D-مغلق E-حریة F-صدیق
G-خروج H-سلام ا-مفتش

Exercise 5

B(i), C(v), D(ii), E(iv), F(vii), G(vi), H(xi), I(x), J(ix),
K (viii)

Exercise 6

Alphabetical order of Arab countries, reading from right to left:

الاردن- البحرین- المغرب- الیمن- تونس- سوریا- قطر- لبنان-
لیبیا- مصر

Exercise 7

Alphabetical order of Arab capitals, reading from right to left:

ابوظبی- الخرطوم- الرباط- الریاض- بغداد- بیروت- دمشق-
صنعاء- طرابلس- عمان

Exercise 8

A(v), B(iv), C(i), D(ii), E(iii)

Exercise 9

A(iv), B(v), C(iii), D(ii), E(i)

Exercise 10

A-٨٠	B-٢٠٠	C-٧٠	D-٩٦	E-٢
F-٤٠	G-٤	H-٩٥	I-٢٢	J-٣٥

Exercise 11

A(vi), B(iv), C(vii), D(i), E(ii), F(iii), G(v)

Exercise 12

A- بيت B- سوق C- سهم D- نور E- خطر F- ممنوع G- جامعة H- صغير
I- القاهرة J- أوتوبيس K- جبل L- حفلة M- سكوت N- صحراء O- صديق
P- كلام Q- عائلة R- مغلق S- مشكلة T- فاكهة

Exercise 13

B- يوم سعيد C- البحر البعيد D- جبل عالى E- طفلة شقية F- بيت قديم
G- المديرة الجديدة H- حجرة نظيفة I- الدور الثانى

Exercise 14

B- المطعم الغالى C- الرجل اللطيف D- القهوة الساخنة E- إمرأة لطيفة
F- الشارع الضيق G- الأخ الغنى H- الحجرة المغلقة I- تذكرة رخيصة
J- العصير الطازج F- الصديق الوفى

Exercise 15

Missing word: عربى

Afterword

Congratulations, you have just learned the Arabic alphabet!

You have studied 28 letters, the hamza, vowel marks, numerals, and how to form the feminine. You have also been introduced to handwritten Arabic. By now, you should have a solid grasp of the Arabic script and feel confident enough to read and write basic words. You can now begin developing your vocabulary and learning basic grammatical structures. Remember, practice makes perfect, so continue by copying examples of Arabic writing you see in magazines, newspapers, books, etc.

Where will you go from here? It's up to you to decide!

It all depends on the degree of Arabic proficiency you want to achieve. You may want to continue with classical Arabic studies, learn the culture, learn to read and communicate, or just understand simple signs and instructions. You are now empowered with a strong basis of the Arabic script.

Good luck!

مع أطيب الأمنيات

The Arabic Alphabet

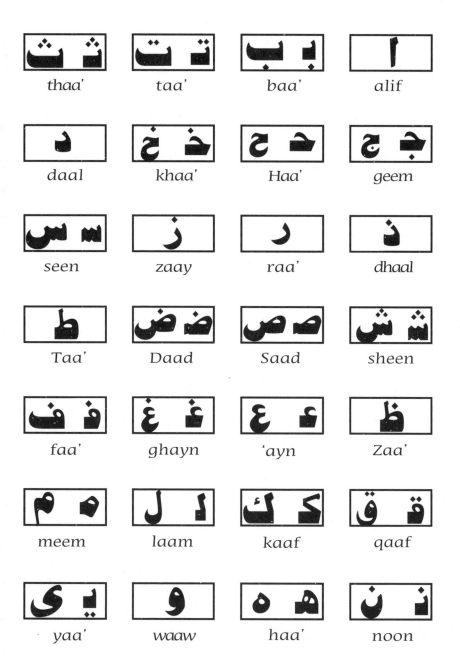

thaa'	taa'	baa'	alif
daal	khaa'	Haa'	geem
seen	zaay	raa'	dhaal
Taa'	Daad	Saad	sheen
faa'	ghayn	'ayn	Zaa'
meem	laam	kaaf	qaaf
yaa'	waaw	haa'	noon

Arabic is written from right to left, this workbook opens on the other side. It was designed this way to help you get used to the Arabic format of writing.

About the Author

Naglaa Ghali is a journalist and English/Arabic interpreter. She has devoted much of her own time to developing funwitharabic.com, an online program that uses a fun approach to learning Arabic. Ghali's approach helps learners of the Arabic language overcome the sometimes challenging and overwhelming intricacies of the Arabic script. In this new workbook, *Write it in Arabic,* Ghali extends that same principle to paper and provides students with hands-on experience in writing Arabic.

To learn more about Ghali and *Fun with Arabic,* visit her Web site at *www.funwitharabic.com.*